Meditation
for Kids

Meditation for Kids

How to Clear Your Head and Calm Your Mind

JOHANNE BERNARD AND LAURENT DUPEYRAT

ILLUSTRATIONS BY ALICE GILLES

bala kids

boulder 2019

BALA KIDS
An imprint of Shambhala Publications, Inc.
4720 Walnut Street
Boulder, Colorado 80301
www.shambhala.com

9 8 7 6 5 4 3 2 1
First U.S. Edition
Printed in China

♾ This edition is printed on acid-free paper that meets the
American National Standards Institute Z39.48 Standard.
♻ Shambhala Publications makes every effort to print on recycled
paper. For more information please visit www.shambhala.com.
Bala Kids is distributed worldwide by Penguin
Random House, Inc., and its subsidiaries

Designed by Liz Quan

LIBRARY OF CONGRESS CATALOGING-IN-PUBLICATION DATA
Names: Bernard, Johanne, author. | Gilles, Alice, illustrator.
Title: Meditation for kids: how to clear your head and calm your mind /
Johanne Bernard and Laurent Dupeyrat; illustrations by Alice Gilles.
Other titles: J'ai rendez-vous avec le vent, le soleil et la lune. English
Description: First U.S. Edition. | Boulder: Bala Kids, 2019. |
Audience: Age 8–12.
Identifiers: LCCN 2018048579 | ISBN 9781611806205 (pbk.: alk. paper)
Subjects: LCSH: Meditation—Juvenile literature.
Classification: LCC BF637.M4 B46813 2019 | DDC 158.1/28—dc23
LC record available at https://lccn.loc.gov/2018048579

To all people, big and small,

who practice meditation and keep it alive

Contents

PART ONE

What Is Meditation?

· ·

All of the moon and
the sky fit comfortably
in a dewdrop.

—Zen koan*

*A koan is a riddle
used to reveal
profound truths to
Zen Buddhist
practitioners during
meditation practice.
And it is through the
practice of meditation
that the meaning of
a koan is revealed!

Where Does Meditation Come From?

Meditation is very ancient, so ancient that we do not really know when it first started. But based on the first meditation writings, the Vedas, we can say that the practice of meditation is at least 3,500 years old.

The Vedas come from ancient India. They are sacred teachings that were written down in Sanskrit, one of the oldest languages in the world and still studied today. The word *veda* means "knowledge" in Sanskrit.

The practice of meditation is found in almost all religious traditions and looks different in each of those traditions. It may involve concentrating the mind, contemplation, repetitions of sound or verbal expressions, dancing, and so on. The types of meditation we will focus on in this book also come from India and appeared about 2,600 years ago. That was the time that a man known as the Buddha lived and taught. It was from his teachings that Buddhism was born. And we will be following in his footsteps.

Conditions have changed a lot since the time of the Buddha. Meditation has spread far and wide across the world, but it has never lost its roots. Today, it is still possible to practice meditation as it was practiced in the time of the Buddha.

Traditionally, meditation is often practiced in groups (for instance, by monks or nuns in monasteries). But some people, such as renunciates, have practiced meditation by withdrawing from everyday life. For instance, in the past some Christian ascetics, the stylites, meditated their whole lives on the top of stone pillars without ever coming down! Renunciates called *yogis*, who follow the example of the Buddha, sometimes practice alone in forests or in the mountains or in caves. There are still many yogis today, some meditating deep in Himalayan forests, some on the banks of the Ganges, the most sacred river in India, and some even in cities. But for many of us, there is no need to go find caves or monasteries to meditate in. All we need is a nice place to sit. And there is also no need for us to choose whether to meditate alone or with other people—we can do both!

Who Was the Buddha?

Meditation is an important practice of Buddhism, which is both a religion and a philosophy, inspired by the teachings of the Buddha. Buddha (which means "awakened one") was born in the sixth century B.C.E. But before he was the "Buddha," he was called Siddhartha Gautama, which means "he who reaches his goal."

Siddhartha Gautama was the prince of a small kingdom in the north of India, near the border with Nepal. Like all princes, Siddhartha was supposed to succeed his father, King Suddhodana. He was kept secluded within the palace and knew nothing of the miseries of the world. It was not until he was thirty years old that he managed to leave the palace. It was then that he discovered for the first time the existence of old age, sickness, and death. This was a big shock for the prince. How was it possible for suffering like this to exist? More than anything, the prince wanted to find an answer to this question, so Siddhartha left the palace and his wife and child and went off alone into the forest to meditate on himself and on the world. He was determined to find out what the origin of suffering was and how to put an end to it. For more than six years, Siddhartha lived in the forest far from everything, hardly eating. He observed his mind and tried to understand how it worked: Why did he think? Why did he have sensations, emotions? Why was he happy or unhappy?

After years of training in this way, he finally succeeded in discovering some profound answers to some of these questions, but he still was unable to find the answer to his main question. So, he decided to leave the forest and sit at the base of a certain fig tree in the meditation posture known as the "lotus position," and he vowed not to get up from that spot until he had discovered the true root of sufferings. Under this tree, the Bodhi Tree, in the north of India, Siddhartha attained enlightenment—which is another way of saying that he discovered the true nature of all things. It was at this moment that the prince became the Buddha, or the Awakened One. The Buddha went on to devote his whole life to teaching what he had learned through meditation: the path to enlightenment, the end of all suffering. He passed away at the age of eighty.

The Bodhi Tree is located in Bodhgaya, in the north of India. This *ficus religiosa*, which is thirty meters tall, has heart-shaped leaves and is still visited today by Buddhists.

What Is Meditation?

Meditation is a training of the mind that teaches you to closely observe your internal world. It is both a practice and at the same time a way of being: by being present in a natural way to everything that happens in you, you will get to know a lot of things about yourself that you didn't know before—it will make you an explorer of your inner world!

What Do You Observe in Meditation?

In meditation you observe anything that stirs you up—thoughts, emotions, sensations, and so on. You look at them the way you look at clouds passing in the sky—without judgment. Whether your sensations are pleasant or unpleasant doesn't actually matter very much. If you feel joy or pain within you or outside of you—the heat of a fire or the coolness of the wind, for example—you just notice it: "Hmm, it's warm." "Hmm, it's cold." "Hmm, I feel happy." "Hmm, I feel sad." And then you let this thought pass away like a balloon flying away in the sky.

How Does It Work?

To be able to observe yourself, two qualities are necessary: attention and concentration.

Attention makes it possible to focus directly on anything at all and to keep observing it without thinking, very simply. In the beginning, that will only last for a few seconds, because you will very quickly forget to observe. That's where concentration comes in—this is what makes it possible for you to remain attentive for a long time, sometimes even for hours, without being bothered by anything else.

In the Buddhist tradition, we call this attentive concentration "mental calm," and the idea is to do it effortlessly—that is, without forcing it.

Meditation uses tools like breathing, physical posture, and sound to help you attain the experience of attention. In the beginning, you have to concentrate to find out how to be attentive. Then, through repetition, you begin to feel more and more comfortable with this state. You naturally become attentive to what is happening in you and you do it effort-lessly. At that point, effortless attention becomes continuous attention. Then there is no longer any need to occupy your mind with what you are supposed to be doing—it happens all by itself! This is very practical, as it simplifies your life. You tend to be calmer no matter what is happening, and you are more present to what you are doing, so you can also do more things at once.

Why Do We Talk about Training in Meditation?

The more they train, the better and better violinists get at playing the violin. And the more they train, the better and better athletes get at their sport. In the same way, the more you meditate, the easier it will become for you to be attentive and concentrate without effort, and the more present, alive, and relaxed you will become. With practice, you will expe-rience joyful attention and concentration. Meditation helps you in all the things you do in life, and it might just help you play football or practice the violin too!

Sensations, Thoughts, and Emotions

When you get good or bad news or are in a situation you're
not used to, you often only notice the emotion this causes—
maybe fear, happiness, anger, sadness . . . But if you really look
at what is happening, you see that before the emotion happens, many other things happen. First, there is often a physical sensation (a tightening in the throat, a knot in your
stomach, trembling in the legs . . .). Then comes a thought
("Oh, my throat has tightened up," "Oh, I've got a stomach-
ache," "Wow, my legs are shaky"). The emotion only arrives
after all that ("I'm scared," "I'm angry," "I'm sad").

So, the emotion is the result of a sensation plus your thought
about the sensation. The emotion does not exist by itself. In
meditation, the attention you develop makes it possible for
you to recognize the sensation for what it is and to stop the
process of having it develop into an emotion right at the
beginning. For example, if you ever come face to face with a
big spider and your whole body shrinks back, because of
meditation you will be able to say, "Hey, my body is shrinking
back." And then that's the end of it. Without thinking, "I'm
scared," you just relax again, and you can continue on your
way—and so can the spider!

Emotion is the result of a sensation plus our

hought about the sensation.

Meditation and the Brain

We often think that meditation is an activity in which we neither move nor do anything else. In reality, it's quite the opposite. Even though it may seem from the outside that nothing is happening, a lot is going on in our brain!

Researchers have studied this question to find out what happens in the brain when we meditate. They studied the brain activity of people who were meditating by placing electrodes on their skulls to measure the electric activity of their brains. They then performed MRI scans, a procedure that enabled them to see in color the areas of the brain that were activated as the people meditated.

They made the discovery that meditation had the ability to physically transform the brain. Certain parts of the brain that were normally isolated from each other became connected with each other during meditation. And more amazing still, they found that certain regions of the brain became bigger as the result of meditation practice. This is why meditation is called training the mind. As with an athlete training the body, certain areas of the brain, stimulated by meditation, become more muscular.

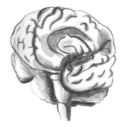

Areas of the brain activated by meditation

The result? More attention and a greater ability to concentrate. But also, according to the scientists, meditation has other beneficial effects on the body, such as slowing down the aging of cells, relieving stress, and strengthening the immune system and the heart, to name a few.

Will knowing all this have much practical effect on your efforts at meditation? Not really. In order to meditate, all you have to do is settle down in your place, and the rest will take care of itself! But our understanding of the ways that meditation affects the brain has created many changes in the field of health. For example, doctors are starting to recommend meditation as a way for people to manage pain. And that is only the beginning of what researchers are learning!

How Do You Get Started?

Where?
To meditate properly, you first have to find a quiet place, because meditation is done in silence. You don't talk during meditation!

It could be done inside: in your bedroom or in any room in your house or apartment where you can be completely alone. It can also be done outside: in your backyard or in a park where there's not too much noise. It's important for the place to not be too warm or too cold when you begin to meditate—you should be as comfortable as possible.

For How Long?
The time you spend can vary from one meditation to another, but on average you should meditate for 5 minutes as you are getting started. When you have repeated some of the exercises in this book and have gotten into the habit of meditating, you can move on to spending 10 or 15 minutes. The most important thing is not how long you meditate—the most important thing is to be really mentally "there" during your practice. We call this "being present."

What Do You Need to Meditate?
You really don't *need* anything to meditate. But the following checklist suggests a few things that might be helpful to you at the beginning.

CHECKLIST

A cushion . . . to make yourself more comfortable sitting on the ground.

A timer . . . so your mind doesn't have to keep track of how much time is left in each exercise!

A small blanket . . . just in case you get a bit cold or to help support your back if you're going be sitting in meditation for a longer time.

A glass of water . . . in case you're thirsty after your exercise.

Your pet . . . but only if it can stay quietly at your side without expressing its joy in meditation too much! After all, we have to stay focused.

Posture: What's the Right Position?

Meditation can be practiced either with movement or without movement. Whether you meditate sitting or standing up, moving or without moving, the principle of meditation always remains the same: attention and concentration.

When you meditate without movement, you train more on concentrating in a fixed way with your attention focused. Meditating with movement, you train on concentrating in a more dynamic way with your attention open. That's why it is said that meditating sitting down or standing up are both equally important!

Before taking the meditation posture, you should always begin by taking off your shoes so that you are as comfortable as possible.

Sitting Posture

In the sitting posture, you sit either cross-legged on the ground or, for greater comfort, on a cushion. Your back is straight, and your head is tilted a bit down. Your mouth is closed. Depending on which meditation you are doing, your hands are either

1

- resting on your knees, palms down (see figure 1) or

- resting in the space between your crossed legs, with the back of your right hand on the palm of your left hand (see figure 2).

2

Your gaze is directed toward the floor just in front of you. It remains focused there for the entire length of the meditation session. You breathe naturally.

Traditionally in Buddhism, this posture is called the "lotus position," because the legs crossed this way resemble a lotus flower.

Do people in your family want to learn to meditate too? Your whole family can join in these meditation practices if they'd like, so there are instructions for teaching your parents these meditations too. Sometimes sitting on the floor is too difficult for parents. They may get pains in their legs. If that's the case, they can sit in a chair. Their legs should be parallel and their feet flat on the floor. As for the rest (the position of the hands, the back, the gaze, the breathing), it's all the same! (See figure 3.)

3

Standing Posture

In the standing posture, your legs and your feet are held right against each other, side by side. Your back is straight, and your head is in the same position as in the sitting posture: tilted slightly downward. Depending on which meditation you are doing, your hands are either

4

- hanging by your sides, with your palms facing your thighs (see figure 4) or

- one on top of the other at the level of the heart: the right hand, turned downward, grasps the thumb of the left hand (see figure 5).

5

Your gaze rests on the floor just in front of you. It should remain that way for the entire meditation. Just keep breathing like you normally do.

The Cherry Tree in the Garden Meditation

To begin a meditation properly, first you have to try to settle down. Like a jar of water with sand in it that has been shaken up, our mind can be stirred up by thoughts and emotions. When that's the case, it's hard to concentrate! If the sand can gently settle and come to rest on the bottom of the bottle, the water can become clear again. In the same way, beginning a meditation by settling down makes it possible to see more clearly into your mind. An exercise we call "the meditation of the cherry tree in the garden" helps us do just that—this visualization is great for calming down and for starting our practice, whether we're going to do a sitting meditation or a meditation with movement.

What Time of Day?
Do the cherry tree visualization before you begin any sitting meditation or meditation with movement. Do it any time of day (if you're going to do just this on its own).

For How Long?
1 minute.

How Many Times per Week?
Do this every time you do a meditation exercise— ideally, at least two or three times a week.

What Is It Good For?

Using the visualization of the cherry tree in the garden, this meditation helps make your head feel light and your body feel firmly grounded in the earth.

This basic meditation helps you to begin all meditation exercises in the best of conditions so that you are grounded and centered. This exercise is great before doing any number of things—like concentrating on your homework or playing your favorite sport!

THE PRACTICE

....

The first important thing to do is to make sure you are set up properly: You should be sitting cross-legged on the floor with your back straight and your head tilted slightly forward. In this meditation, the palms of your hands rest quietly on your knees. Your gaze is focused on a point in front of you on the floor. Remember to breathe naturally.

All ready? Off you go for 1 minute of being a cherry tree in the garden!

With your gaze focused on a point in front of you near the floor, first place your attention on the lower part of your body: feel how you are resting firmly on the floor, well-rooted and stable, like the cherry tree in the garden with its very deep roots anchored in the earth.

Do you feel that your roots are quite solid? Now move your attention to the upper part of your body, which is quite light and seems to want to take off upward,

like the branches of a tree reaching for the sky.

At the end of the meditation, you should feel two different sensations: a stability below that gives you strength and a lightness above that gives you joy.

You are like the cherry tree in the garden—solid and radiant.

Teaching Your Parents to Meditate

Once you have been practicing the cherry tree meditation for at least two weeks, you will be ready to teach it to your parents!

First, begin by explaining to your parents how to properly set themselves up.

Show them the posture they should take, and don't forget the most important thing: their gaze

should be fixed on a point on the ground in front of them. Check to make sure everyone is in the right position.

Next, explain the different sensations of the cherry tree meditation to them: feeling the lower part of your body well rooted in the ground and then feeling the upper part of your body light like the leaves of a tree.

Has everybody got it? Then you're on your way to having a family orchard of cherry trees! And of course, remember, the orchard should be silent . . .

PART TWO

Sitting Meditation

· · · · · · · · · · · · · · · · · · ·

The wind has
no hands, and yet it
shakes the trees.

—Zen koan

Wind Meditation
Meditating on the Breath

In the wind meditation, you are going to observe your breathing so that you can begin to learn how to tame it. Just as the wind stirs the branches of a tree, the air that comes into and goes out of your body brings life and also stirs your body up as much as your thoughts and emotions do. By concentrating on your out-breath and your in-breath, you are going to start learning about your inner rhythm . . .

What Time of Day?

Do the wind meditation in the morning, either when you wake up or right after breakfast. You can also do it in the late afternoon or evening: when you come home, before doing your homework, or before going to bed.

For How Long?

5 minutes: 1 minute for the meditation of the cherry tree in the garden plus 4 minutes for the exercise with the breath.

How Many Times per Week?

Do this as many times a week as you want, but only once a day.

What Is It Good For?

The wind meditation lets you become aware of your natural rhythm. Breathing is the basis of life, and breathing well is essential for living well . . . But your breathing is also the mirror of your emotions: When you are frightened, your breathing speeds up. When you are relaxed, you breathe more slowly.

By training yourself to concentrate on your breathing, you can become aware of your inner state faster. If your breathing speeds up and you're not running, for example, it means you're experiencing an emotion that disturbs you. Remembering how to breathe calmly during the exercise will make it possible for emotions to calm down by themselves.

This meditation helps you to settle down, and if you do it in the morning, it will enable you to stay more focused the whole day long.

THE PRACTICE

....

Are you ready for a big breath of air? Go for it!

Seated on the ground or on a cushion, begin with 1 minute of the meditation of the cherry tree in the

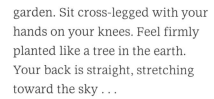

garden. Sit cross-legged with your hands on your knees. Feel firmly planted like a tree in the earth. Your back is straight, stretching toward the sky . . .

Is the minute over?

Staying in the same position, close your mouth and breathe only through your nose. Keep your mouth closed for the whole length of the exercise—except of course if you have a stuffed nose! In order to concentrate better, also keep your eyes closed during the whole exercise.

Now with your mouth and eyes closed, place your attention on your breath: breathe in slowly while being aware of the air coming into you.

And don't forget: always begin with the cherr

Teaching Your Parents to Meditate

You can feel how the air spreads through your body—for example, how your lungs swell and how your rib cage opens up.

Hold your breath for one or two seconds . . . then breathe out slowly. Here too, during the out-breath, try to feel where the air passes through your body, how your belly contracts, and how your lungs empty out. Continue in the same way, concentrating alternately on the air coming in, the air being held, and the air going out. Do this for 4 minutes.

Now it's time to open your eyes. Without moving, direct your gaze a little downward and effortlessly keep it steady on one point.

That's it! All done. You can get up now.

Have you been practicing the wind meditation for a month? Then now is the time to teach it to your parents.

Begin by getting your parents comfortably settled on cushions on the ground or in chairs. Then, sit facing them on a cushion so you can explain the exercise to them. Is everyone seated and concentrating properly? Begin your explanation of the wind meditation by showing them what they have to do: breathing in, holding the breath for two seconds, then breathing out.

To get your parents to understand clearly, accompany your explanation with sounds and movements: breathe louder than usual and at the same time make small movements with your head—upward for the in-breath, downward for the out-breath.

Summarize the whole exercise again and check to make sure everyone has understood . . . Wind meditation is a breeze!

ree in the garden meditation.

The Meditation of the Sun and Moon
Meditating on Sensations

In our next meditation, we are going to make use of two heavenly bodies that you know well—the sun and the moon—in order to explore the sensations of heat and coolness that their light brings us. Like breathing, light has a big influence on our lives and on the lives of all living beings. Plants need light to survive, and we do too . . .

By visualizing the sun and moon and concentrating on their light, you are going to come to know the pleasant and gentle sensation that these two heavenly bodies bring.

What Time of Day?

Always do the meditation of the sun and moon in the morning—preferably after having had your breakfast and just before you get started on the rest of your day.

For How Long?

5 minutes: 1 minute for the cherry tree in the garden meditation, plus 2 minutes for the visualization of the sun, plus 2 minutes for the visualization of the moon.

After six months of practice, if you have time, you can move on to doing 9 minutes: 1 minute for the cherry tree in the garden meditation, plus 4 minutes for visualizing the sun, plus 4 minutes for visualizing the moon.

How Many Times per Week?

Do this as many times a week as you want, but only once a day.

What Is It Good For?

Learning to connect with sensations that are good for you will enable you little by little to bring extreme sensations that pass through you into balance.

Like our planet, which can't survive without the alternation of the sun and moon, we humans also need the dynamic energy of the sun and the peaceful energy of the moon alternating with each other. When you visualize the golden beams of the sun, warmth and joy arise naturally. You will notice that your sensations become more vivid. When you visualize the silvery rays of the moon, coolness and gentleness emerge and calm your sensations. By repeating these experiences, you will begin to understand how to call upon the energy of the sun or the energy of the moon, depending on which one you need.

When you feel tired or a little depressed, you can concentrate on the sun to get back your strength and your sense of joy in being alive. When you feel very excited and your emotions are too strong, you can concentrate on the moon to soothe yourself and calm yourself down.

The Meditation of the Sun and Moon
THE PRACTICE
....

Are you ready for some sunbathing and moonbathing? Let's go!

Seated on the ground or on a cushion, begin with 1 minute of the meditation of the cherry tree in the garden. Sit cross-legged with your hands on your knees, firmly grounded like a tree in the earth. Your back is straight, stretching toward the sky . . .

Since you are going to work with your imagination, (in order to concentrate better) close your eyes.

Your breathing is natural. Your eyes are closed. Now imagine the sun just in front of you, with no sky and no clouds. It is very brilliant and shines majestically with a golden light that warms you. This beneficial warmth floods your body and gives you energy, strength, and joy. Stay still and contemplate this for 2 minutes.

The sun disappears.

Now visualize the full moon in front of you, with no sky and no clouds. Silvery white, radiating a soft light, the moon soothes you and makes you feel peaceful. It feels good—cool and pleasant— after the heat of the sun. Remain peaceful in the soft light of the moon for 2 minutes.

Then, very slowly, the moon disappears and you remain there without imagining anything for a few moments.

Now you can open your eyes and get up. You're done!

It's important to do this meditation in this order for a month: first the sun, then the moon. After doing this practice for a month, you can decide for yourself which heavenly body to begin with. For example, if you're too warm, you can begin with the moon. If you feel a bit sad, you can start with the sun.

Teaching Your Parents to Meditate

Have you been practicing the meditation of the sun and moon for two weeks? Then it's time to teach it to your parents!

Begin by getting your parents comfortably settled on cushions on the ground or in chairs. Then, sit facing them on a cushion so you can explain to them properly what they have to visualize: first the sun, then the moon. Explain clearly about the sensations of warmth and coolness that these heavenly bodies bring us. You can also tell them not to worry about wearing sunglasses or putting on sunscreen. Here there's no risk of sun stroke or moon stroke, because the light comes from inside.

Is everybody ready? Off we go to bathe in the sun and the moon together!

Meditation on a Stone
Meditating on a Physical Object

The basic principle of the meditation on a stone is concentration. By fixing your gaze on an object, you will learn to focus your attention. Focusing in this way will allow you to develop your concentration. The more focused you are, the more attentive you will be, not only to what you're looking at but also to everything surrounding you. Your attention will become more open. That is what is called a virtuous circle!

What Time of Day?
Do the meditation on a stone anytime!

For How Long?
5 minutes: 1 minute for the meditation of the cherry tree in the garden plus 4 minutes for the meditation on a stone.

After one month of practice, if you have time, you can move on to doing 9 minutes: 1 minute for the meditation of the cherry tree in the garden plus 8 minutes for the meditation on a stone.

How Many Times per Week?
Do this as many times a week as you want.

What Is It Good For?

If you're like a lot of kids, you probably have a hard time concentrating. You have lots of things to do, lots of screens to look at, all kinds of activities you're involved in . . . You probably don't make time just to be quiet, not even for 5 minutes. When you meditate on the stone, not only will you be taking 5 minutes to slow down, but you will also be getting the benefit of strengthening your attention. At the beginning, it might seem difficult to concentrate on a stone and let all your thoughts go by, because you have a lot of thoughts! But as you continue to repeat the exercise, you will find it increasingly easier, and going back and gazing at the stone will become something you enjoy! Staying focused on a single object will make it possible for you to tidy up your mind a bit, and you'll learn to let your confusing, jumbled up thoughts just go on by.

THE PRACTICE

For our next practice, you need a stone. Find a stone that you find pretty and nice to look at—not too small and not too big . . . You can always use the same stone, or you can use a different one each time—as long as you don't spend too much time picking them out!

Have you found your stone? Just keep it handy to begin with . . .

Seated on the ground or on a cushion, begin with 1 minute of the meditation of the cherry tree in the garden. You sit cross-legged with your hands on your knees, firmly grounded like a tree in the earth. Your back is straight, stretching toward the sky . . .

Is the minute over? Take the stone and put it on the ground in front of you at a distance of about one arm's length. Now place your hands in the space between your crossed legs. Your hands should be flat, with the back of your right hand on the palm of your left. Fix your gaze on the stone and let your thoughts come. Do you find the stone pretty? Good. Let that

thought pass. Do you think you should have cleaned the stone up more to make it shinier? Good. Let that thought pass. Does the shape of the stone seem weird? Good. Let that thought pass . . . Stay like that for 4 minutes, concentrating on the stone. Now gently lift your gaze and stretch your legs. You're ready to get up. You're done!

Teaching Your Parents to Meditate

Have you practiced the meditation on the stone for two weeks? In that case, the time has come to teach it to your parents.

For this meditation, each person should have his or her own stone. You can ask your parents to bring their own stone along—or you can pass out a stone to everyone before starting.

Begin by getting your parents comfortably settled on cushions on the floor or in chairs. Then, ask them to put their stones on the ground in front of them, about an arm's length away. Explain to them that the goal of the exercise is to stay focused on the stone while letting thoughts pass by without becoming attached to them—and of course, not saying them out loud! And remind them that each person should focus on the stone in front of them and not on their neighbor's.

Is everyone as well-behaved and motionless as their stone? The meditation can begin!

The Lemon Peel Meditation
Meditating on a Taste

Here, you are going to focus on one of the five senses—the sense of taste. Have you ever tasted pure lemon—that is, lemon zest (peel) or lemon juice with no sugar added? If not, try biting into a slice of lemon sometime! For in this meditation, relying on your memory, you're going to recall the sharp sensation of lemon on your tongue along with its acidic flavor. This is a meditation for those who are adventurous with their sense of taste.

What Time of Day?
Do the lemon peel meditation in the morning or in the evening before eating. This will stimulate your appetite!

For How Long?
5 minutes: 1 minute for the meditation of the cherry tree in the garden plus 4 minutes for the lemon peel meditation.

How Many Times a Week?
Do this as many times a week as you want.

What Is It Good For?

This meditation will help you learn how your senses
work. Through experiencing the taste of lemon
without a lemon, you will realize that your inner sense
does not always have to be connected with an object—
the lemon—but it can be connected with your memory
of an experience—the experience of having eaten
some lemon. The point is, your sensation can be
produced by a thought alone, by a thought that is
influenced by a memory. You will see that your mind
is capable of re-creating anything, even if the object
is not physically present. It will become clear to you
that it is possible to re-create a sensation just by
concentrating. What a good way to have fun with
your senses!

THE PRACTICE

....

Ready to thrill your taste buds? Try some lemon!

Seated on the ground or on a cushion, begin with 1 minute of the meditation of the cherry tree in the garden. You sit cross-legged with your hands on your knees, firmly grounded like a tree in the earth. Your back is straight, reaching for the sky . . .

Now close your eyes and try to concentrate in order to bring back the taste of lemon. Lemon is sharp on the tongue. It's a little harsh on your throat when you swallow. It can give you the shivers. It might be helpful to imagine biting into a slice of lemon, but don't forget to concentrate only on the taste of the lemon, not on its color or its form.

Teaching Your Parents to Meditate

Is your mouth watering? That's a good sign. That means the meditation is working.

So, keep concentrating on the taste of lemon for 4 minutes. If you lose the taste of lemon, you can restart by imagining a few drops of lemon on your tongue. Is your mouth watering again? That means that you're concentrating again on the memory of lemon. After 4 minutes, you can open your eyes and get up. All done!

Although this meditation is called the lemon peel meditation, after a week of practicing it, you could also try it with any other fruit, or even try mixing different flavors together . . .

Have you been practicing the lemon peel meditation for two weeks? Now is the time to teach it to your parents.

Begin by getting your parents comfortably settled on cushions on the floor or in chairs. Then, sit facing them so you can describe the exercise to them. Explain to them that they will be concentrating on remembering the taste of lemon. To make the importance of the sensation really clear to them, you can make faces to show how sharp the taste of a lemon is on the tongue. You can also let them know that if their mouths are watering, that's normal and it's a good sign, but they should be careful not to drool.

Is your family of taste chefs ready? Then let's do it!

Little Stories about Sitting Meditation

Buddhism has a custom of handing down many little traditional stories about meditation. They tend to be funny a lot of the time, but nevertheless they give us real teachings on how to practice. Here are two that are adapted from Zen* stories, involving students and their meditation teachers.

> A meditation student went to see his teacher and told him, "My meditation is terrible! I'm very distracted, and my legs hurt, or I'm constantly falling asleep. It's really horrible!"
>
> "It will pass," his teacher said.
>
> A week later, the student went back to see his teacher. "My meditation is fabulous," he told him. "I'm completely mindful, peaceful, and full of energy. It's terrific!"
>
> "It will pass," his teacher replied.

This little story teaches us that there are no successes or failures in meditation. Meditation has no goal as such. It can be different every time—sometimes pleasant, sometimes unpleasant. The important thing is settling down and doing the exercise, not getting a particular result.

Here's a story about a very old meditation teacher and a young student:

> The young student asked his teacher, "Tell me, O great teacher, how long will it take me to become a great meditator?"
>
> The teacher thought for a while and then replied, "Thirty years."
>
> The student, disappointed, replied, "Oh no, that's really a long time!

---

* Zen is a type of Buddhism that started in China under the name Chan and developed in Japan with the name Zen.

What if I work really hard at it, think about nothing else day and night, and practice very hard? How long will it take me then?"

The teacher thought for a while longer than he had the first time, then replied, "In that case—fifty years."

Yes, it's true, for meditating, working really hard doesn't help! The only effort you have to make is to remain genuinely attentive, but that really has to be a joyful, light, and natural effort. It really doesn't matter how long it takes you to reach a state of concentration. Again, it's not the result that counts, but doing the practice.

And finally, here's a little story about monks who are having a very hard time not talking during meditation.

> In a small temple in a very remote place in the mountains, four monks were doing *zazen*.* They made up their minds to do a session in absolute silence. It was late, and they had only one candle for light.
>
> Sitting properly in their postures, they meditated and reached a state of concentration . . . But after a short time, the candle went out, plunging the room into darkness.
>
> The youngest of the monks said in a hushed voice, "The candle just went out!"
>
> The second monk replied, "You shouldn't talk. It's supposed to be a totally silent session."
>
> The third one said, "Why are you talking? We're supposed to be silent and not talk!"
>
> The fourth one, who was in charge of the session, was clearly proud of himself as he replied to the other three: "I must point out that I'm the only one who didn't say anything."

* Zazen is the main meditation practice of Zen.

PART THREE

Meditation with Movement

Where does the light go when I turn it off?

—Zen koan

The Tightrope Walker's Meditation
Walking Meditation

Walking is an activity that comes quite naturally. Without thinking about it, we lift one foot after the other and we move forward that way, a little bit like robots. The fact is, we are not really aware of what is happening when our body moves, nor of what is making it move.

In the tightrope walker's meditation, you are going to do a very simple thing: walk on an imaginary straight line while paying close attention to everything that is happening within you with each movement of your body. Like an astronaut getting a first glimpse of the moon, you will move along your line in slow motion so you can observe clearly how everything going on inside you works.

What Time of Day?
Do the tightrope walker's meditation anytime. Inside, or outside if you're prepared for the weather.

For How Long?
5 minutes: 1 minute for the meditation of the cherry tree in the garden, plus 3 minutes of slow walking, plus 1 minute of being calm without movement at the end.

How Many Times per Week?
Do this as many times a week as you want, but don't do it more than once a day.

What Is It Good For?

This meditation will teach you how to remain very focused while performing an action—in this case, walking. It will also enable you to realize that your thoughts and emotions keep working at the same time as all the parts of your body do.

By training yourself to walk like a tightrope walker, little by little you will become aware of the way your body moves and of what makes it move. Before your body moves, you have the idea of moving. Then, your body goes into motion. Doing this exercise slowly, you will be able to see that your movements are influenced by your thoughts and emotions. For example, you will notice that if you lose your concentration and begin thinking about something else, you can easily lose your balance between two steps, and your breathing will speed up. What is most important to observe here is the way the various aspects of you— your breathing, the movement of your body, and the movement of your thoughts—work with each other.

THE PRACTICE
....

All meditations begin with the meditation of the cherry tree in the garden. But please note, with certain meditations the cherry tree meditation is done standing. As in the sitting version of the cherry tree meditation, your head is tilted slightly downward and your gaze is focused on a point on the ground in front of you.

Are you ready for this experience? Forward march!

Stand, either barefoot or wearing socks, with your feet together and your arms at your sides, palms against your thighs. Begin now by doing the standing meditation of the cherry tree in the garden for 1 minute, feeling your feet firmly rooted in the ground.

Now lift your hands to the level of your heart and with your right hand turned downward, grasp the thumb of your left hand. Close your left hand over your right.

Then, hold your hands against your chest, but not too tightly.

With your head tilted slightly forward, keeping your eyes focused on the ground in front of you, begin to walk, *veeeery slooooowly*, following an imaginary straight line in front of you. It is important as you're walking to notice all the parts of each move-ment clearly.

Train yourself by moving forward step by step. First lift your right foot, then bring it forward, until you can plant your heel slowly on the ground. Once your heel is down, pause briefly. Still slowly, place the rest of your foot flat on the ground, while at the same time lifting your left foot onto the toe. Pause again.

Then gently lift your left foot and plant the heel a step ahead, while keeping your right foot still quite flat on the ground. Pause again.

Teaching Your Parents to Meditate

Now, at the same time as you are placing the rest of your left foot on the ground, lift your right foot onto the toe, and pause once more. Finally, slowly place the heel of your right foot on the ground ahead.

Repeat this process for 3 minutes. Don't forget to do each movement very slowly. Just as though you were walking on the moon, every movement is gentle and slow.

To finish, bring your feet together again and end the exercise the way you started it, lowering your arms again to your sides and concentrating in a simple way for 1 minute—with your gaze directed in front of you, without moving, keeping your attention on your breathing.

That's it! You've done it!

Have you been practicing the tightrope walker's meditation for one month? Then now's the time to teach it to your parents.

Begin by arranging everybody in a standing position in a room. Pick a room big enough so people don't bump into each other while walking.

Stand facing your parents so you can explain the different stages of the meditation by clearly showing them the movements of the walk: placing the heel down, pausing after each step . . . Don't hesitate to do it even more slowly than usual so they can understand it quite clearly. You can even ask them to do it once for you, so you can make sure that they have all the movements right.

Is everybody ready?

It's time to do the meditation all together.

Place everybody in a row with you in front. That way everybody will be able to time their step to yours. When you lift your right foot, the person behind you will lift the same foot, and so on down the line. It's a meditation caterpillar!

The Clock Meditation
Meditating on Turning around Yourself

In our next meditation, you are going to turn around yourself the way the hand of a clock does. By changing the direction you are facing by quarter turns, with each turn you will see the space that surrounds you from a different angle. Like a watchman in a tower, who can include the whole landscape in one glance, you will become aware of the space around you as a whole by looking at it from different points of view.

What Time of Day?

Do the clock meditation following an afternoon snack during the week or following breakfast on the weekend.

For How Long?

6 minutes: 1 minute for the meditation of the cherry tree in the garden plus 5 minutes for the clock meditation.

How Many Times per Week?

Do this four times a week at the most. It doesn't matter which days.

What Is It Good For?

This meditation will teach you to be aware of the space around you. It will show you that even if you change position, the space around you as a whole still stays the same. In the same way, no matter what angle you are looking from, your way of being attentive and concentrating also does not change. Finally, you see that there is a kind of stability within the movement: your body moves, but the space and your attention stay the same. By repeating this exercise, you can train yourself to remain stable in the midst of movement. Being stable in the midst of movement will help you to remain stable through all the changes that happen in your life. Because life is movement!

THE PRACTICE

Are you in position for your trip around the clock? Ready, go!

Stand, either barefoot or wearing socks, with your feet together and your arms at your sides, palms against your thighs. Begin now by doing the standing meditation of the cherry tree in the garden for 1 minute, feeling your feet firmly rooted in the ground.

Now lift your hands to the level of your heart and with your right hand turned downward, grasp the thumb of your left hand. Close your left hand over your right. Then, hold your hands against your chest, but not too tightly. Keep your hands at the level of your heart during the whole exercise.

Raise your head so you can look straight ahead. Keep your gaze steady and straight ahead, and become aware of the whole room or the whole place where you are.

Teaching Your Parents to Meditate

Keep your gaze steady and remain quiet like that for 1 minute. Now make a quarter turn to the right, and take the same position, keeping your gaze straight ahead, for another 1 minute.

Make another quarter turn to the right. Now you are facing in the opposite direction from the direction you were facing at the beginning. Keep your gaze steady and straight ahead of you, becoming clearly aware of the space you are in for 1 minute.

Make another quarter turn to the right, and there again, for 1 minute keep your gaze steady, straight ahead of you. Finally, make a last quarter turn to the right, which brings you back to your initial position. Now repeat the exercise one last time for 1 minute.

There, the trip around the clock is finished! You can let go of your posture and relax.

Have you been practicing the clock meditation for two weeks? Then the time has come to teach it to your parents.

Begin by placing everybody in a room in a standing position, leaving each person enough space to turn around in without disturbing his or her neighbor.

Then explain the principle of the meditation: turning around yourself while keeping your gaze steady and becoming aware of the space around you. In order to show them clearly how to do this, you can mimic the hands of a clock, explaining to them that when they make a quarter turn, it's a quarter after the hour. When they turn twice, it's half past. When they turn three times, it's a quarter to. When they go all the way around, it's smack on the hour. And then you're finished!

Is everybody in place? Then let's begin to turn like the hands of a clock.

The Meditation of the Pink Flamingo
Meditating on Your Sense of Balance

Like pink flamingos who stand on one leg so they can rest while they're sleeping, with this meditation you're going to work on your balance—but you will also become especially aware of how your thoughts influence your body. This is an exercise that seems very simple, but it has so much to teach us!

What Time of Day?
Preferably, the meditation of the pink flamingo should be done late in the day—after school or after your afternoon snack, for example.

For How Long?
5 minutes: 1 minute for the meditation of the cherry tree in the garden plus 2 minutes on your right leg and 2 minutes on your left leg.

How Many Times per Week?
Do this four times a week at the most.

What Is It Good For?

In this meditation, you will discover that your thoughts influence your movements quite a bit. What does that mean? It means everything is connected. We don't have our thinking in one place and our body in another. Everything is linked and works together. So, if you want to have your body working well, you also have to have your mind working well. You will realize, for example, that when you are calm and focused, you can hold your posture very well. On the other hand, when your mind is agitated, you quickly and easily lose your balance. So, by repeating this exercise, you're going to learn little by little to keep all the different aspects of yourself in balance: your body, your thoughts, your sensations, and your emotions. In the beginning that may seem difficult, but after a while, it happens all by itself!

THE PRACTICE

....

Let's work toward a real sense of balance. Here we go!

Stand, either barefoot or wearing socks, with your feet together and your arms at your sides, palms against your thighs. Begin now by doing the standing meditation of the cherry tree in the garden for 1 minute, feeling your feet firmly rooted in the ground.

Now, lift your hands to the level of your heart and with your right hand turned downward, grasping the thumb of your left hand, raise your head so as to look straight in front of you, and lift your right leg. Now stay in this position for 2 minutes. Be careful; this is not easy in the beginning. But if you lose your balance, it's not serious. You can simply take your posture again. It's just as important to stay properly focused, to keep your gaze steady, and to be aware at the same time of the space you are in and of what is happening in your body. Once the 2 minutes are up,

put your right leg down. Now lift your left leg and repeat the exercise for 2 minutes. At the end of the exercise, put your left leg back down on the ground. That's it, you've got both feet back on the ground! You can relax. All done.

Teaching Your Parents to Meditate

Have you been practicing the meditation of the pink flamingo for two weeks? Then the time has come to teach it to your parents!

Begin by placing everybody in a standing position, either barefoot or in stocking feet. Make sure that the room is big enough so there's enough space for people to lose their balance without bumping into each other.

Then stand facing them so you can show them how to balance on one foot and then the other. Point out clearly that thoughts have an effect on balance, and be sure that everybody understands this. Also let them know that if they lose their balance, it's nothing serious. They just have to retake the posture they were just holding . . . The hardest thing will be for people not to laugh at each other and lose their balance as a result. If you're not careful about that, the whole exercise will just turn into a big falling-down party!

Remind everybody clearly that the meditation of the pink flamingo is mainly all about concentration.

So now the pink flamingo family is ready for its journey on one foot. Happy balancing!

Meditation on O
Meditating on Sound

....

Next, we have a meditation in which you're going to concentrate on sound, particularly on the vowel *O*, a round sound that completely fills space. By sounding a long *O*, you will become aware of the impact your voice has on your body and mind. When we sing, our thoughts take flight . . . Like the breath, sound—which is carried by our breath—resounds everywhere within us and around us.

What Time of Day?

Preferably the meditation on *O* should be done in the morning, before leaving for school or doing any other activity.

For How Long?

5 minutes: 1 minute for the meditation of the cherry tree in the garden plus 2 minutes for the meditation on *O* and 2 minutes of silence.

How Many Times per Week?

Do this as many times a week as you want!

What Is It Good For?

This whole meditation is especially good for dissolving thoughts, and for the last 2 minutes, it is good for being very present, calm, and peaceful. It also allows you to see how your breath affects the way you sing and also affects the sound itself. The *O*, when you pay attention properly, resounds everywhere within yourself and makes everything vibrate. Once again, you realize that everything is connected and that everything within you is working together at the same time.

THE PRACTICE

Are you ready for a long O? Let's get those vocal cords working!

Seated on the ground or on a cushion, begin with 1 minute of the meditation of the cherry tree in the garden. You sit cross-legged with your hands on your knees, firmly grounded like a tree in the earth. Your back is straight, stretching toward the sky . . .

Then, staying in that position, just wait quietly for a little while, without trying to do anything.

Teaching Your Parents to Meditate

Now go ahead and make the sound O, holding it for the longest possible time without forcing it and without shouting. When you run out of air, stop.

Wait a little while and begin again, concentrating attentively on the sound and the vibrations it produces.

Try to feel where the sound comes out and what effects it has.

Make this sound of O several times in the course of 2 minutes. Then stop.

Remain quietly in your position without doing anything for 2 minutes more.

All done. You can get up.

Have you been practicing the meditation on O for two weeks. Then the time has come to teach it to your parents!

For this meditation, it's a good idea to pick a large room in the inner part of the house where you can hear sound the best. Place everybody in a circle, seated on the floor, and explain the exercise, stressing the fact that there are two parts to this meditation: the first part when everybody makes an O sound, and a second part when everybody remains silent. You can make a long O sound to show them how to do it—not too soft and not too loud—and tell them not to forget to begin breathing again when they run out of breath. And everybody doesn't have to make their O sound at the same time. Each person should find his or her own rhythm.

Is the family choir ready to go? Let's get started with our O symphony!

A Little Story about Meditation with Movement

Often meditation stories speak for themselves—
just as in practicing meditation, no commentary is
necessary . . .

Here's a story about meditation with movement.
Remember meditation means being present every
moment, no matter what you're doing . . . Even
while you're reading a story about meditation!

One day some people asked a man who was a good
meditator how he kept so calm and focused despite all the
things he was busy doing. He replied:

"When I get up, I get up.
 When I walk, I walk.
 When I sit, I sit.
 When I eat, I eat.
 When I talk, I talk."

The people interrupted him, saying, "We do the same
thing! What else do you do beside that?"

The man was silent for a moment, and then he replied:

"When I get up, I get up.
 When I walk, I walk.
 When I sit, I sit.
 When I eat, I eat.
 When I talk, I talk."

Again the people said to him, "Yes, that's what we do too."

"No," he told them:

"When you're sitting, you're already getting up.
 When you get up, you're already running.
 When you're running, you think about sitting down.
 When you sit down, you think about eating."

PART FOUR

Meditation on the Cycles of Nature

· · · · · · · · · · · · · · · · · · · ·

A man looks
at a flower;
the flower smiles.

—Zen koan

Meditation on the Weather

Meditating on Your Immediate Experience

Now we're going to do a meditation in which you will make use of something that is always with you, every day of your life: the weather. You will learn to observe how the weather outside influences you inside. How? By opening your window wide and making use of your ability to look and feel. Then, when you're sitting down, you will make use of your memory and your imagination. In this way, you will be able to make contact in the present moment with the rays of the sun, with snowflakes, or with falling rain . . .

What Time of Day?

Always do the meditation on the weather in the morning—preferably after you have had breakfast and just before you start the rest of your day.

For How Long?

5 minutes: 1 minute for the meditation of the cherry tree in the garden plus 4 minutes for the meditation on the weather.

How Many Times per Week?

Do this every day of the week if you like, but always do it in the morning and not more than once a day.

What Is It Good For?

The meditation on the weather enables you to realize that if you are really present, every moment you are alive is incredibly vivid!

Is it raining today? Would you rather have had nice weather? In meditating on rain, you will see that we're really lucky to have rain. If you are constantly wishing for something else or always wanting more, it's because you are not at all aware of what is actually happening right where you are, in the present moment. If you are always wanting something else, you are never satisfied with your life. Through this meditation, you will discover that you can enjoy every moment without trying to make it into something different.

By repeating this exercise, you will also learn how to relate to the weather outside in a more natural way. You will always be more present to the changing of the seasons and more sensitive to the atmosphere. You will find out how not only your body but also your emotions are connected to the climate outside. You shiver when it's cold, sweat when it's hot, are happy when it's springtime, and get nervous when there's lightning . . . In a way, you will rediscover that you are living on earth and that everything is connected to everything else!

THE PRACTICE

Are you ready to stick your nose out and sniff the weather? Let's go!

Before starting, go to the window, open it for just a few seconds, and smell what kind of air you are getting this morning.

Is it warm or cold? Is it a nice day? Is it snowing? Maybe it's raining . . .

Whatever kind of weather you find, immerse yourself in the atmosphere by closing your eyes for a moment. Then, close the window and go and sit down.

Seated on the ground or on a cushion, for 1 minute do the meditation of the cherry tree in the garden. You sit cross-legged with your hands on your knees, firmly grounded like a tree in the earth. Your back is straight, stretching toward the sky . . .

Then close your eyes and try to remember what you were just feeling by the window.

Is it fine and beautiful out? Experience again the softness of the air, the rays of the sun caressing your face, the birds singing in the trees.

Or is it snowing? Experience again the gentle cold on your skin and how silent it is outside. Experience

Teaching Your Parents to Meditate

the snow falling and the faint noise it makes. . . .

If you like, you can let your imagination carry you away and go gather pollen from the flowers along with the butterflies or take a walk through the crunchy snow. But the most important thing for you to do is feel the atmosphere of today's actual weather (not the weather you might wish you were having) and to remain quite focused on that.

Remaining inside, sitting with your eyes closed, concentrate in order to re-create the atmosphere you experienced at the window. Do this for 4 minutes.

You're done now. It's time to open your eyes. Stay there for a little while with your eyes directed downward, focused on one point, but without effort. Now you can get up and go to the window and have a look at the weather again.

Have you been practicing the meditation on the weather for two weeks? Then now is the time to teach it to your parents!

For this meditation, choose a room with at least one big window that can be opened, because each person is going to go take a turn at it.

Ask your parents to sit down so you can explain the principle of the meditation to them—that is, the idea is to retain in the mind the feeling of the weather outside. Open the window and have them sniff and experience the feeling of the weather outside. People can go to the window one at a time or all together if the window is big enough.

You can tell them to close their eyes so they can feel the weather more completely. Once everybody has had a turn at the window, close it and ask everybody to be seated again on their cushion or chair. Go over the steps of the meditation one more time with them, and check to make sure everybody has understood it properly . . .

Then it's off to explore the atmosphere!

Meditation for the End of the Day
Meditating on What Is No Longer There

....

For the next meditation, once more you're going to
make use of your imagination. But this time your
imagining is going to be based on your memories. This
will be a meditation on "what is no longer there":
you're going to meditate on all the things you've done
during the day that has just passed. At least all the
things you can remember! By meditating this way, you
will see how much your memories determine the way
you act, talk, think, and live in the present moment.

What Time of Day?

Always do the meditation for the end of the day in the
evening—ideally, just before you go to bed.

For How Long?

5 minutes: 1 minute for the meditation of the cherry tree in
the garden plus 4 minutes for the meditation for the end of
the day.

How Many Times per Week?

Do this every day of the week, if you like, but only in the
evening and not more than once a day.

What Is It Good For?

By meditating on your memories, you will be training yourself to develop your attention and your memory, but also in this meditation you will review all the pleasant and unpleasant events you have lived through over the past day. This will enable you to gain a clearer awareness of the things you did and said—whether they have worked out for the best or not. Which ones do you regret? Which ones made you unhappy? And on the other side, which ones brought you a feeling of joy and well-being? Going back over what happened during the day from the point of view of how you experienced it inwardly allows you to see clearly what you really want for yourself and for other people. That clarity will help you make good decisions so you won't have to regret anything, and you will be able to take full advantage of all the moments of your life before they go by.

Through this meditation, you are going to realize that once your day is over, you will never have a chance to live through it again. The passing away of time is part of everyone's experience, whether they are young or old. This is one of the realities of our lives. You don't have to be frightened about it. Just the opposite is true. Fear of the passage of time often comes from the fact that people have many regrets about things. Recalling your experiences will enable you to appreciate your life without those feelings of fear or regret. Little by little, you will become more keenly aware of your natural inner time—not the kind of time that is defined in minutes and seconds, but the kind of time that is naturally your own. Being perfectly in harmony with that inner sense of time, you will naturally be in harmony with yourself!

Meditation for the End of the Day
THE PRACTICE

....

Are you ready for a little journey through your memories? Let's go!

Sit on the floor or on a cushion, and begin with 1 minute of the meditation of the cherry tree in the garden. Sit cross-legged with your hands on your knees and your gaze focused on a spot on the ground in front of you.

Now, staying focused on that spot, try to remember the day that has just gone by. Do that for the next 4 minutes.

First try to remember your morning. How did you wake up? How did your breakfast go? What happened after that? If you didn't have school today, what happened at home? If it was a school day, what happened on the way to school? What happened during class and recess? Then, remember your lunch break, who you ate with, what you talked about . . . What did you learn in class after lunch? Who did you talk to or what games did you play?

Finally, remember the later part of the day. Remember what happened when you got home. Did you have a snack? What else happened . . . while you were doing your homework? while you were just taking it easy? while you were having dinner with your family? To the extent that you can remember what took place, your memories pass. They fly away like colored balloons and make room for the ones that come next—and in their turn, those fly away too.

Do some memories get stuck and linger? Or on the other hand, are there certain things you don't want to remember? Are there things that happened that you don't like? Is there something you did or said that you now regret? If that's the case, concentrate directly on the sensation created by that memory and let it pass.

You can take advantage of having had that memory to ask yourself what it was about it that upset you: was it something you said or did yourself, or was it something that came from somebody else?

Teaching Your Parents to Meditate

After you remember what it was that upset you, simply let the memory go, once again like a balloon flying away and disappearing in the sky.

When the 4 minutes are up, just stop focusing on the spot in front of you and take a moment or two to relax and stretch.

You can get up now. All done!

Have you been practicing the meditation for the end of the day for one month? Then the time has come to teach it to your parents!

Get everybody set up comfortably on a cushion on the floor or in a chair. Then, sit down facing them so you can explain to them what they're supposed to do: Remember what happened during the day. Look at the feeling that each experience brought. Then, let the memories fly away like colored balloons in the sky. You can give them an example, like breakfast. Ask them if they can remember what happened at that time. Don't forget to also tell them to concentrate on the feelings they have in connection with memories that linger . . . until those memories fly away in their turn like balloons. That way, there will be no regrets.

Has everybody understood? Then it's memory time. Ready, set, go!

Meditation on the Circles of the Universe
Meditating on the Space around Us

....

When a stone is thrown into the water, it creates bigger and bigger circles that ripple out from the center. In the same way, in the meditation here, by concentrating, you are going to open your perception to what is around you and try to develop a bigger and bigger view that takes in more and more things. Relying on your imagination, you will be able to go farther and farther out . . . even as far as the most distant galaxies!

What Time of Day?

Do the meditation of the circles of the universe in the morning, either when you wake up or after breakfast.

For How Long?

About 10 minutes: 1 minute for the meditation of the cherry tree in the garden plus about 9 minutes for the meditation on the circles of the universe.

How Many Times per Week?

Do this three times per week.

What Is It Good For?

This meditation will help you to realize what your real place in the universe is. By making a small effort to concentrate, you will see that you are not isolated, not all alone in your little corner. But you are also not the center of the universe! You are going to be able to see that the reality within which you are growing and developing is truly vast and that everything within it is connected.

By repeating this exercise, you will become aware of the importance of everything around you—living beings as well as objects and landscapes. You will realize that all things are present at the same time, in the same reality, and that everything is important for the life of everything else. What would the sky be without the stars? What would you be without your parents? Could humans exist without all the other things in the natural world? As you find your own place in the universe through this meditation, kindness and compassion toward yourself and everything else will emerge in you!

THE PRACTICE

....

Are you ready to take a great journey? Are the seatbelts on your explorer's ship properly fastened? Then let's go!

Sit on the ground or on a cushion, cross-legged, with your back quite straight and the palms of your hands resting flat on your knees. Now begin with 1 minute of the meditation of the cherry tree in the garden.

Close your eyes and start by imagining yourself in the room that you're in. Then, enlarge your circle of concentration, the way a stone thrown into a pond makes bigger and bigger circles around it in the water. Now try to imagine your house and everybody in it. Don't forget your pets if you have any! Then enlarge the circle again and imagine the neighborhood your house is in, with all its inhabi-tants—your friends if there are any living nearby, and maybe your parents as they are shopping at the grocery store or working at the office . . . Make a bigger circle and

imagine your whole part of the country, with all its inhabitants, its different landscapes, the animals in it, the construction sites, the machines, the cars, the trains, the planes . . . Make another circle, and now imagine the whole country with all its towns and cities, all of its different regions, and all its inhabitants. Make one more circle, and you've got the whole of the Americas, with many countries north and south—with lakes and forests, rivers and mountains, pine trees and palm trees, rocky coasts and sandy beaches . . . Well done! Now the next circle puts you in orbit around the earth. You see our planet as a whole, with its people, its animals, its various landscapes, its lakes, its rivers, its seas, its oceans . . . Then, you are up there with the sun and the moon and the planets of the solar system. You want to go farther still? Do you have enough time? If so, the next circle will take you way out there among all the galaxies . . . It's really a very big universe!

After you've come to the outer edges of the galaxies, it's time to come back down in the opposite direction, slowly and calmly, until you find yourself once again in your room—which you never left. The journey is over now. You have taken a tour of the whole universe in 9 minutes!

Now open your eyes and focus your gaze for a second or two in a downward direction. All done! You can get up!

During the exercise, you can stop in any one of the circles. You can also take your time making your circles bigger—no need to become the world's greatest astronaut on your first try. And if you would enjoy spending more time in any one of the circles than in the others, that's fine too. You just have to pay attention to the time. You only have 9 minutes for your trip through the universe.

Teaching Your Parents to Meditate

Have you been practicing the meditation of the circles of the universe for one month? Then the time has come to teach it to your parents!

Start by getting your parents comfortably seated on a cushion on the floor or on a chair.

Then sit down facing them so you can explain to them what they have to do.

Is everybody seated and concentrating? Then explain the meditation of the circles of the universe to them. Be careful to point out all the stages: the first circle, the second circle, the third circle, and so on.

You can use lots of details. Describe clearly what they have to imagine. That way your parents will be able to tell what level they're on with each circle.

Summarize the whole thing once again and check to make sure that everybody has understood properly . . . The family ship is on its way. Fasten your seatbelts!

The Long Meditation of the Cherry Tree in the Garden

Meditating between Earth and Sky

....

To conclude the exercises in this book, we will practice a meditation that should only be done outside in a place in nature that feels beautiful to you—in the garden of your house, in the neighborhood park, or in the woods where you take walks with your family . . . This meditation is based on something you have become very familiar with: the cherry tree at the back of the garden! Now you are going to go a little bit further in exploring this exercise.

What Time of Day?

It doesn't matter when you do the long meditation of the cherry tree in the garden, but *always* do it outside.

For How Long?

8 minutes: 4 minutes for the first part plus 4 minutes for the second part.

How Many Times per Week?

Do this as many days a week as you want, but not more than once a day.

What Is It Good For?

You are familiar with the cherry tree visualization as something valuable that you do at the beginning of every meditation. It is calming and stabilizing. It makes it possible for you to be naturally present, because it teaches you to let go. The advanced phase of this meditation, which you are going to do here, not only retains these qualities but also enables you to concentrate on your natural physical condition—we are continuously on the ground and under the sky.

Effortlessly become aware once again of the ground under your feet and of the sky over your head. Doing this reminds you of the importance of keeping a balance between the two. In the end, life is like meditation. In your practice with the meditations in this book, you have seen that concentration helps you to open up your attention. In the same way, feeling yourself to be well rooted in the ground helps you to open up to the endlessness of the sky . . .

THE PRACTICE

....

Is the sky blue? Are your feet enjoying the fresh air? Then go ahead with 8 minutes of the cherry tree in the garden.

In a standing posture, barefoot or wearing socks, direct your gaze downward toward a point near the ground and keep it steady. Immediately raise your hands to the level of your heart.

Then, to begin with, place your attention on the lower part of your body. Try to feel quite clearly that you are standing on the earth, that you are well settled on the ground, quite stable. Concentrate on the sensation of solidity beneath your feet. Try to stay with this without moving for 4 minutes. Don't forget to pay attention as strongly as possible to the fact that you are stoutly rooted in the ground.

This meditation is always done outside, preferably in a beautiful spot on a nice day when the sky is clear. If you are in the grass, don't hesitate to take your shoes off. If you are barefoot or just have socks on, you will feel the ground much better! If it's very sunny you can wear sunglasses to protect your eyes—and stand with your back to the sun to avoid being dazzled by it.

Are your roots now quite solid? Then lift your gaze toward the sky.

Teaching Your
Parents to Meditate

Have you been practicing the long meditation of the cherry tree in the garden for one month? Then it's time to teach it to your parents.

Gaze at the sky without focusing on anything in particular. Then, place your attention on the upper part of your body, which feels very light and like it wants to take off upward, like the branches of a cherry tree reaching for the sky. Try to stay that way without moving for 4 minutes.

While you are concentrating on the sky, don't forget that your feet are strongly rooted in the earth. Stay that way, letting all thoughts just pass by and concentrating on the sensation of solidity down below and the sensation of openness and presence up above.

Have 8 minutes gone by? Bring your gaze back downward and relax. The meditation is over. You can go for a walk!

Is it a nice day? Has the whole family decided to go for an outdoor excursion? Then it's the ideal moment to teach your parents the long cherry tree meditation. To begin with, ask everybody to take their shoes off. Place everybody in a semicircle facing you. Now explain the two stages of the meditation to them. Explain that first of all they should concentrate on the sensation of solidity in the lower part of the body and then on the sensation of lightness in the upper part of the body. Make it clear to them that it is important to pay attention to feeling the ground with their feet. You can show them how to do this by making a point of pressing your feet into the ground. Also don't hesitate to exaggerate the movement of your head up toward the sky so they understand quite clearly what they're supposed to do. Tell them not to look straight at the sun when they raise their gaze to the sky. And have those who have sunglasses put them on!

Is everybody standing with their hands at the level of their heart? Is everything clear to everybody?

Then begin. The whole family between earth and sky!

Little Stories about Meditating on the Cycles of Nature

....

Many traditional meditations are intended to help us discover or rediscover our natural state. Here we call these meditations "meditations on the cycles of nature." What is your natural state? Very simply, it means to just be. But this means to "just be" while also being clearly aware of your condition—aware of your place in the universe and on this earth, aware of the fact that your life and the life of everything around you can't help but flow into each other, and aware also of the fact that you are here, with your feet on the ground and your head in the sky, on top of the hill, very naturally . . .

Here are two little traditional stories about the "natural state." They illustrate what it is better than talking about it could!

A long time ago in China, there was a water carrier who had to walk many miles every day to fill his two buckets from the river. He carried the buckets the way people used to carry them in the old days, on the ends of a wooden stick, with one bucket hanging down on each side of him. The water carrier never complained. Quite the opposite—he was always very happy to be coming back from the river with his buckets full of water, in spite of their weight. But still, there was a problem. By the time he got all the way home, one of his buckets was always only half full. It had a leak in it. Every day, the water carrier's lord and master pointed to the half-full bucket, and he beat the water carrier and called him a good-for-nothing. And the poor water carrier would just head back to the river again . . .

One day the leaky bucket couldn't stand this situation anymore because it felt so guilty. It spoke to its owner and said that it could no longer bear seeing the poor water carrier bravely face the dangers of his journey but still only come back with part of the water and be beaten as a result. All because of itself . . . The water carrier looked at his leaky bucket with tenderness for a long moment and then said: "I have been working very hard bringing water from the river for years. My life is not a happy one. But haven't you noticed that when we are on the way back, I'm always smiling and happy?

Why? Because on the side of the road where you are, there is lots of green grass and beautiful flowers of all colors. All that is only because of you. If you didn't have a leak, there would be no flowers and my life would be sad. So I will never exchange you for another bucket or have you repaired, because the way you are is priceless."

In China in the seventh century, there was a man standing alone on the top of a high hill. Three brothers traveling together were passing nearby. They saw the man standing, alone and without moving, on top of the hill. They wondered what this man was doing.

The oldest one said, "Without a doubt he is looking for a lost pet." The second brother said, "No, he must be looking for a friend of his." The third brother said, "Certainly not—he's just peacefully enjoying the fresh air." Not being able to agree among themselves, the three brothers decided to go ask the man.

When they got to the top of the hill where the man was standing, the first brother asked him, "Excuse me, are you standing alone without moving on top of this high hill because you lost a pet?"

The man answered, "No, sir, I didn't lose one."

The second brother asked, "Is it because you have lost a friend?"

The man answered, "No, sir, I haven't lost one."

The last brother asked, "Aren't you just enjoying the fresh air?"

The man replied, "No, sir."

The three brothers cried out, "Why, then, are you there?"

The man standing alone without moving on the top of the high hill said, "I'm just here."

Conclusion

> If the problem has a solution, there's no reason to get upset.
> But if there's no solution, getting upset won't change anything.
>
> —Buddha

All these practices are now part of your life. You can call upon them whenever you wish. Each practice has its own special qualities—it's up to you to choose, day by day, the one that suits you best. Above all, don't forget that meditation is basically a game of discovery, always to be played with enthusiasm, curiosity, and joy. You'll be curious to keep making new discoveries and you'll want to keep experiencing the joy those discoveries bring!

Have fun meditating! Because meditation is not difficult or complicated. It only requires you to be steady and attentive when you practice. There's no need to meditate for hours and turn yourself into a statue covered with dust. A few minutes a day, being very present to what you are doing, is all you need. The more you practice meditation, the more natural it becomes. It fits into your daily life without your having to push or force it. If you make a small effort at the beginning to get yourself to meditate, you will see that more and more it will become a pleasure to go back to.

Meditation is good for you. It helps you to live your daily life better, more openly, and more peacefully. There's nothing out of the ordinary about this—meditation is not a magic formula that takes away all your problems.

In fact, it shows you only that there's nothing to push away or reject. The Buddha said that if you want to help the people you love or help make the world a better place, you have to start by helping yourself. And that's what meditation is for. Meditation is about discovering all the things you can do for yourself and other people and about learning to live without fear and with kindness.

Over many centuries, generation after generation of children and grownups have experienced the many benefits of meditation. They have gained concentration, attention, and an attitude of kindness toward everybody and everything around them. They have gained clarity, peace, and calm . . . These are the main things that only 10 minutes of practice a day can bring you. Not bad, eh?

Shall we end with a very well-known little story?

> One day as the Buddha was sitting on the ground about to give a teaching to a large crowd of people who had come to hear him, he picked a flower that was growing near him. He looked at it for a long time, turning it in his fingers. He didn't say a word. Among all the many people in the crowd, only one began to smile. This was Mahakashyapa, one of the Buddha's main students, and the only one who understood his teaching that day.
>
> That teaching was the essence of meditation!

🌸 Happy practicing! And remember, meditation is simplicity. When you meditate . . . you meditate.

Questions and Answers

What Can Happen when I Meditate?

Many things can happen during meditation! You can have all kinds of feelings and sensations. You can experience images, sounds, lights, memories, and so forth. You might feel very good or you might feel restless. Usually, the more you meditate, the more calm, attentive, and focused you become. Nevertheless, there are days when you will be more restless, when you will experience more moving around, more thoughts, sensations, and emotions. That's normal. Meditation only works if it is repeated—without forcing it. There's nothing to fear about anything that might happen during meditation. Feeling good or feeling restless—it's all natural. Little by little, you will get accustomed to all of the sensations that can happen during meditation. Once that happens, you will never worry about them again!

What If I Have Ants in My Pants and Really Want to Move Around?

That happens often! Don't worry about it. Move around a little bit. Stretch your arms and legs and get back in your posture when the ants are gone.

What If I'm Not Able to Concentrate?

The most important thing is not to force it. If you have the feeling that you just don't have much concentration one day, don't push yourself to meditate. Just end the exercise sooner. Tomorrow will be different!

What If I Fall Asleep?

That's not a problem. It often happens that when people become very relaxed while meditating, they fall asleep. This is because their body interprets the relaxation as the signal to go to sleep. The same thing can also happen if you meditate after eating, because digestion requires a lot of energy and there's not much left over for concentrating. If you fall asleep while meditating, at least you will get a good rest!

Can I Meditate If I'm Sick?

Possibly, but if you're too sick, it's better not to meditate. It might just tire you out rather than focusing your attention.

Can I Meditate with My Pet?

Your pet is welcome if it can behave!

Summary of the Meditations according to Times of Day

	MORNING	AFTERNOON	EVENING
Meditation of the Cherry Tree			
Wind Meditation			
Meditation on the Sun and Moon			
Meditation on a Stone			
Lemon Peel Meditation			
Tightrope Walker's Meditation			
Clock Meditation			

	MORNING	AFTERNOON	EVENING
Meditation of the Pink Flamingo			
Meditation on O			
Meditation on the Weather			
Meditation for the End of the Day			
Meditation on the Circles of the Universe			
Long Cherry Tree Meditation			

Acknowledgments

We would like to express our warm thanks to Florence Lécuyer and Jeanne Castoriano for their enthusiasm and for their confidence in this project; to Béatrice Decroix for bringing us together with Florence and Jeanne; to Garance Giraud for her support from the beginning; and to Alice Gilles for working with patience and humor to give life to the characters in this book. A big thank-you also to all the little meditators who made it possible to try these practices out, and to their parents who urged us to make a book out of them.

Our thoughts also go out to our teachers, whether still with us or already departed . . .